Contents

1 Rainbow plate   2

2 Plant protection!   4

3 The digestive system   6

4 Food and feelings   8

5 Red foods   12

6 Orange foods   14

7 Yellow foods   16

8 Green foods   18

9 Blue and purple foods   20

10 White foods   22

11 Other types of foods   24

12 Colourful meals   26

Glossary   28

Index   29

Which parts of your body are fruits
and vegetables good for?   30

Written by Kathryn Kendall Boucher

Collins

1 Rainbow plate

Fruits and vegetables come in all colours of the rainbow!

They help to keep your body and your mind in great shape.

Fruits and vegetables aren't the only types of food you should eat, but they are a tasty place to start!

Plants make their own food. They use light from the sun, **nutrients** from the soil and water to grow.

sunlight

growth

nutrients →

water →

We, as humans, can't make our own food like this. Instead, we get our energy and nutrients from the food we eat. Nutritious food helps us to be healthy.

2 Plant protection!

Fruits and vegetables contain **phytonutrients** (say *fight-oh-new-tree-ents*). Phytonutrients give plants their colour, protect them from diseases and keep them healthy. Phytonutrients can help to keep *you* healthy, too!

Things like **pollution** from cars, cigarette smoke, or some fats in food can damage our bodies. Some phytonutrients protect our bodies from damage. These phytonutrients are called **antioxidants**.

Fruits and vegetables also contain:

- vitamins
- **minerals**
- natural sugar
- **fibre**.

Vitamins and minerals help your body to grow and to work properly.

Natural sugar gives your muscles and brain energy.

Fibre keeps your tummy feeling full for longer, and makes it easier to poo!

3 The digestive system

Food must be broken down into tiny **molecules** so that nutrients can enter the bloodstream and travel all around the body. This is what the **digestive system** is for.

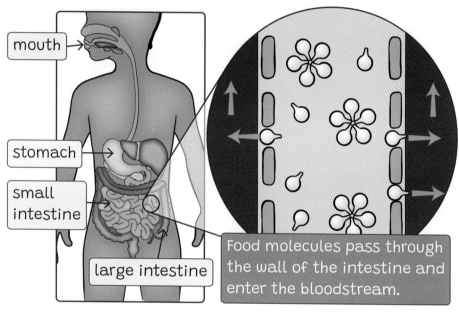

mouth

stomach

small intestine

large intestine

Food molecules pass through the wall of the intestine and enter the bloodstream.

1. Digestion begins when you chew food and it mixes with saliva (spit).

2. Food goes into the stomach, where acid breaks it down further.

3. **Bile** and other liquids in the intestine break food down into molecules that can enter the bloodstream and move around the body.

Nutrients help you to:

- be active
- learn
- grow
- fight illness.

4 Food and feelings

There are billions of neurons (nerve **cells**) in the brain. There are also millions of neurons in the gut. The brain and gut communicate with each other by sending messages along the **vagus nerve**.

If the gut feels irritated or unhealthy, it can send messages to your brain that may make you feel a bit sad or tired. If the gut is healthy, the brain can feel good, too.

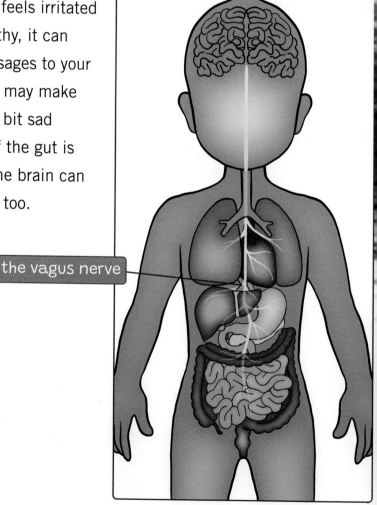

the vagus nerve

Gut bacteria

Your gut contains good and bad **bacteria**.

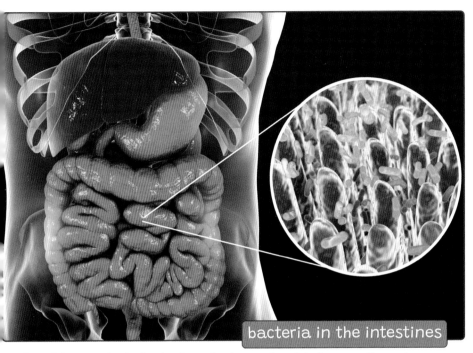

bacteria in the intestines

Good bacteria help to break down food into small parts.
Then you can digest it and **absorb** the nutrients.
Eating healthy food helps good bacteria to grow in
your gut. The more good bacteria that you have, the more
energy and nutrients you can get from your food.

Good bacteria also get rid of bad bacteria in the gut.
If you have too much bad bacteria, you can't digest
food properly.

Food affects mood

Good bacteria produce a chemical called serotonin. Serotonin is known as a "happy **hormone**" because it can put you in a good mood. This is how a happy gut can mean a happy brain!

Did you know?
Up to 95% of your serotonin is made in your gut!

You can't be in a good mood all of the time. It's OK to feel sad, upset or angry. But if you eat nutrient-rich food that is good for your gut, you're setting yourself up to feel more positive.

Some of the best foods for your digestive system are brightly coloured fruits and vegetables.

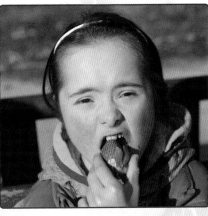

5 Red foods

Red fruits and vegetables get their colour from either lycopene (say *lie-koh-peen*) or anthocyanins (say *an-tho-sy-a-nins*). Lycopene helps to keep your heart healthy and your immune system strong.

Anthocyanins help to protect your brain cells from damage, meaning red fruits and vegetables are also very good for your memory. They can help you remember more of what you learn at school!

strawberries

tomatoes

watermelon

Did you know?
A tomato is a fruit,
not a vegetable!

13

6 Orange foods

Have you ever been told that carrots will help you see in the dark? There is some truth to this old tale! Orange fruits and vegetables are full of **carotenoids**. Carotenoids can help to keep your eyes healthy and stay strong as you get older.

Orange fruits and vegetables help protect all the cells in your body from things like pollution.

You need a mineral called iron for healthy blood. Orange fruits and vegetables help you to absorb iron from other foods.

carrots

Did you know?
Most of the nutrients in carrots are just under the skin, so it's better not to peel them!

peach

sweet potato

butternut squash

15

7 Yellow foods

Yellow fruits and vegetables also get their colour from carotenoids.

They are full of vitamin C, which is great for your skin, hair, teeth and gums. It also helps to build muscle.

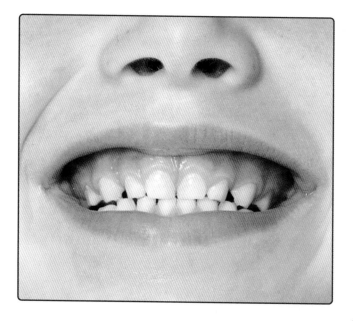

lemon

Did you know?
Lemons can clean things like metal and glass!

mango

pineapple

pepper

17

8 Green foods

Chlorophyll (say *klor-oh-fill*) makes plants green. Chlorophyll is full of phytonutrients.

Green fruits and vegetables also contain **folate**. Folate turns into vitamin B9 when you eat it. Vitamin B9 helps to keep your blood healthy. It also helps a baby's spine to develop properly inside the womb.

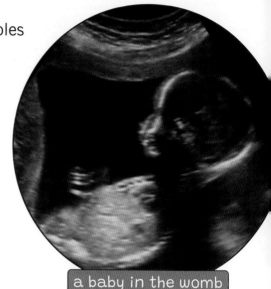

a baby in the womb

grapes

broccoli

Vitamins B9 and B6 are in some green fruits and vegetables. They help to make brain chemicals like serotonin. Having plenty of brain chemicals can help you to feel in a good mood.

Some green vegetables contain calcium (say *kal-see-um*). Calcium is a mineral that keeps your bones and teeth strong, and helps your muscles work properly.

spinach

Did you know?
Some green vegetables contain more vitamin C than fruit!

kiwi fruit

9 Blue and purple foods

Blue and purple fruits are packed full of anthocyanins.

Anthocyanins are good for:

- brain cells
- blood cells
- digestion
- skin
- eyes
- bones.

Blue and purple fruits and vegetables
are often called "superfoods"!

blueberries

blackberries

purple cabbage

Did you know?

You can use purple cabbages to make clothes dye!

21

10 White foods

Not all fruits and vegetables are brightly coloured, but they are still good for you.

Some white fruits and vegetables contain potassium. Potassium is a mineral that helps to keep your muscles moving properly. It also helps to balance the amount of **fluid** in your body.

lychees

mushrooms

potatoes

Did you know?

There are around
5,000 types of potato!

11 Other types of foods

Fruits and vegetables are great.
But there are lots of other foods you
should eat, too!

Grains

Grains are things like wheat, rice and oats. They are
a good source of fibre. Fibre pushes food through your
digestive system and keeps you feeling full.

Your brain uses a lot of energy.
Grains contain carbohydrates, which
turn into a type of sugar in your body.
Your brain uses this sugar for energy.

porridge

Protein

These foods all contain protein.

Protein helps builds bone, muscles, **cartilage** and skin.

fish

meat

seeds

nuts

cheese

eggs

Healthy fats

You might think fat is bad, but that's not always true. Healthy fats give you energy and help you absorb vitamins. Omega 3 is a healthy fat, and it can increase levels of serotonin.

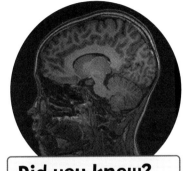

Did you know?
Your brain is mostly made of fat!

avocado

olive oil

salmon

nuts

seeds

Liquids

Liquids keep you **hydrated**. The best liquid is water. Water helps your digestive system to work properly and helps nutrients to travel around your body.

Try to drink six to eight glasses of water a day, especially if it's hot or you've been exercising. You could add fruits for flavour!

12 Colourful meals

Fresh foods are full of nutrients. Some of these nutrients can be lost when we cook them. Many foods, like meat, have to be cooked before we eat them. But if it is safe to eat something uncooked (raw), like an apple or a carrot, you will get more nutrients.

Meals with lots of different food types will be good for your body and your brain. Remember – a happy gut helps a happy brain!

Breakfast ideas

Lunch ideas

Dinner ideas

27

Glossary

absorb to take in

antioxidants things that protect cells of the body

bacteria microscopic living things

bile a yellow/green liquid made by the liver to help with digestion

carotenoids a type of phytonutrient

cartilage stretchy tissue that connects bones and makes up parts of the ear and nose

cells the smallest units of living things

digestive system parts of the body that break down food

fibre a part of food that can't be digested but keeps the digestive system moving

folate a vitamin

hormone a chemical that has a particular effect on your body

hydrated having enough water in your body

minerals substances that come from rock, soil and water

molecules two or more atoms that have joined together

nutrients the food molecules that living things need to be healthy

phytonutrients nutrients from plants

pollution anything that makes the environment dirty

vagus nerve the nerve which controls mood and carries messages between the brain and the heart, lungs and digestive system

Index

anthocyanins 12, 20

antioxidants 5

bacteria 9, 10

bones 19, 20, 24

brain 5, 8, 10, 12, 19, 20, 24, 25, 26

carotenoids 14, 16

chlorophyll 18

digestive system 6, 11, 24, 25

eyes 14, 20

fat 5, 25

feelings 8, 11

fibre 5, 24

folate 18

gums 16

gut 8, 9, 10, 11, 26

heart 12

immune system 12

iron 14

lycopene 12

mood 10, 11, 19

minerals 5, 14, 19, 22
  – calcium 19
  – potassium 22

muscles 5, 16, 19, 22, 24

phytonutrients 4, 5, 18

protein 24

skin 15, 16, 20, 24

sugar 5, 24

teeth 16, 19

vitamins 5, 16, 18, 19, 25
  – vitamin C 16, 19
  – vitamin B6 19
  – vitamin B9 18, 19

Which parts of your body are fruits and vegetables good for?

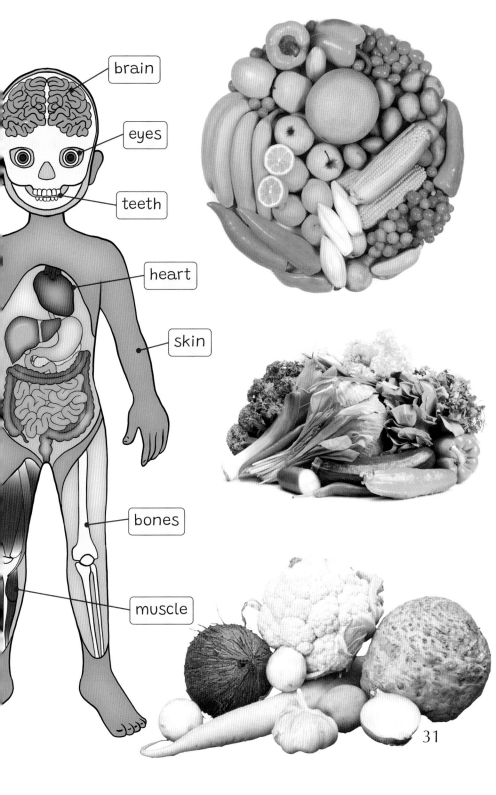

brain

eyes

teeth

heart

skin

bones

muscle

31

Ideas for reading

Written by Christine Whitney
Primary Literacy Consultant

Reading objectives:
- identify and discuss themes in a wide range of writing
- listen to and discuss a wide range of non-fiction
- ask questions to improve understanding of a text
- explain the meaning of words in context
- identify main ideas drawn from more than one paragraph and summarise these

Spoken language objectives:
- participate in discussion
- speculate, hypothesise, imagine and explore ideas through talk
- ask relevant questions

Curriculum links: Science: Animals, including humans: recognise the impact of diet, exercise, drugs and lifestyle on the way bodies function

Interest words: nutrients, pollution, digestive system, bacteria

Build a context for reading

- Read the title of the book without showing the illustration. Ask children to share their predictions about what the book could be about.

- Reveal the image and discuss children's predictions. What do they now believe the book will be about?

- Read the blurb on the back cover. Encourage children to ask a question they would like to see answered in the book.

Understand and apply reading strategies

- Read Chapter 1 together. Ask children to summarise what they have learnt about *nutrients*.

- Continue to read together up to the end of Chapter 2. What is the name for the phytonutrients that *protect our bodies from damage?*

- Read together to the end of Chapter 4. On p10 it says, *This is how a happy gut can mean a happy brain!* Ask children to explain how this can happen. Support them to use the words *bacteria* and *vagus nerve* in their explanations.